Grace Kelly

American Princess

Grace Kelly

American Princess

Elizabeth Gillen Surcouf

Foreword by Frank Sinatra

Lerner Publications Company ■ Minneapolis

Many thanks to the Princess Grace Foundation-USA, Joyce Barnathan, and the Jim Musurca family. I also want to thank my friends and my own family, especially my daughter, Erin—who once wondered if a princess was "just pretend."

Library of Congress Cataloging-in-Publication Data

Surcouf, Elizabeth Gillen.
  Grace Kelly, American princess / Elizabeth Gillen Surcouf.
      p.   cm. — (The Achievers)
  Summary: A biography of the successful American actress who married the Prince of Monaco and became a modern-day princess.
  ISBN 0-8225-0548-7
  1. Grace, Princess of Monaco, 1929-1982 — Juvenile literature. 2. Motion-pictures actors and actresses—United States—Biography—Juvenile literature. 3. Monaco—Princes and princesses—Biography—Juvenile literature. [1. Grace, Princess of Monaco, 1929-1982. 2. Actors and actresses. 3. Princesses.] I. Title. II. Series.
DC943.G7S87   1992
944.9'49—dc20
[B]   92-9626
                                                                    CIP
                                                                    AC

Manufactured in the United States of America

International Standard Book Number: 08225-0548-7
Library of Congress Catalog Card Number: 92-9626

1 2 3 4 5 6 97 96 95 94 93 92

Contents

Foreword

What a marvelous book this is! The life of Her Serene Highness Princess Grace of Monaco is a modern fairy tale. You can almost feel her gentleness, charm, warmth, and poise leap off the pages. This wonderful friend of mine play-acted her way to the top of Hollywood stardom and then put make-believe behind her to become a real-life leading lady when she married Prince Rainier III of Monaco.

Grace's charitable work began during her childhood in Philadelphia and matured in Hollywood. It grew to full bloom in the palace situated high on the cliffs of Monaco, overlooking the Mediterranean Sea. Many of Princess Grace's good works light the pages of this book. Although there isn't space to mention everything she has done for humanity, her joy, her generosity, her love, and her caring nature are unforgettably sketched here. My memory of Princess Grace is that of a very real person who shared her fairy tale with the entire world. Her name reflects the lovely woman she was . . . Grace.

Frank Sinatra

September 1992

Princess Grace wore the national costume of Monaco at the 25th anniversary celebration of Prince Rainier's reign.

1

Childhood

In 1974 Princess Grace of Monaco wanted to celebrate the anniversary of her husband's reign. Prince Rainier had ruled Monaco for 25 years. Grace planned an enormous barbecue for more than 4,000 Monégasques, or citizens of Monaco. She had to hold the party in a soccer stadium, the only place large enough to hold them all. Grace dressed up in a straw hat, a white blouse, and a red and white skirt with a black silk apron—Monaco's national costume. The people at the celebration sang and danced. Prince Rainier played *pétanque,* a French bowling game, with some Monégasques. The successful event gave the people of Monaco a feeling of community.

As a young woman, Grace had been a famous actress before her marriage to a prince. What's more, Princess Grace was an American, born Grace Patricia

Kelly, in Philadelphia, Pennsylvania. Her story sounds like a fairy tale, but it really happened.

Grace's grandparents were poor Irish immigrants. Her grandfather John Kelly was a manual laborer. Her grandmother Mary moved to the United States when she was 13. Like Grace, Mary loved to read. She memorized Shakespeare and enjoyed quoting his works. Her children grew up loving books.

Like many children in the 19th century, Grace's father had to quit school while he was still young. He started working in a carpet mill when he was nine. But Mary Kelly made sure her children found time to read. She encouraged their talents and hard work and taught them that they could achieve anything. Jack Kelly, Grace's father, had been an athlete when he was growing up. He won an Olympic gold medal in 1920 for a type of boat racing called sculling. Grace's uncle Walter, her father's older brother, became a well-paid comedian who traveled around the world. Later Jack started a brickwork company with a loan from Walter.

Margaret Majer, Grace's mother, was a determined woman. She went to Temple University and graduated with an associate of arts degree. This was quite an achievement for a woman in 1920. Margaret became the first woman to teach physical education at the University of Pennsylvania. She coached the university's swim team and even did a little modeling.

Christmas at the Kelly house in 1933 was a joyful occasion. *From left to right,* Peggy, holding Lizanne on her lap, four-year-old Grace, and John, Jr.

Jack Kelly went swimming often. He met Margaret Majer, who was an excellent swimmer, at a pool one day. The two found that they shared athletic interests, and both were ambitious. In 1924 Margaret and Jack decided to marry. The couple had four children. Grace was the third.

A few weeks before Grace was born, the U.S. stock market crashed, and many people lost their fortunes overnight. Banks closed and people lost the money they'd been saving all their lives. Millions of Americans were jobless. Many people became homeless as poverty spread throughout the country. This period, which

The Kelly family in 1936. Left to right are Grace, Peggy, Mrs. Kelly, Lizanne, Mr. Kelly, and John, Jr.

continued into the 1930s, was called the Great Depression.

But Grace Kelly grew up protected from the pain of the depression. She was born on November 12, 1929, into a life of comfort. Her father had risen quickly from poverty to wealth. Grace lived in the house her father had built for the family. The depression made the Kelly family's comfort seem extraordinary. Jack Kelly tried to help as many people as he could by providing bricklaying jobs.

As a child, Grace had a strong imagination and was almost never bored. She pretended her dolls were actresses coming alive onstage. She enjoyed reading quietly in her room—especially Uncle George's plays.

Uncle George Kelly was an actor and a distinguished writer. He won a Pulitzer Prize in 1926 for writing *Craig's Wife*, a successful Broadway play. In some ways, Grace was like her uncle George, a gentle book-lover. She loved to listen to him quote whole scenes from Shakespeare. It was George Kelly who inspired Grace's interest in the theater. She hoped that one day she could act in one of his plays on Broadway in New York City.

When she was 11, Grace saw the Ballet Russe perform. She was inspired to take ballet lessons for two years after that, and later she studied modern dance. Dance led her to imagine herself onstage. It also helped her become more athletic. She was a good swimmer and even became captain of a hockey team.

When she was 10 years old, Grace spent summer vacation in Ocean City, New Jersey.

Seventeen-year-old Grace dances with her father, John Kelly.

When Grace wasn't at school, she practiced acting and worked very hard at "make believe." By the time she was 12, she often performed with the East Falls Old Academy Players. Because she was tall, she looked older than she was. Her mature, calm appearance helped her get many different roles. Some of the other girls giggled as they spoke their lines, but Grace's talent stood out.

Grace was a good student at both Ravenhill Grammar School and Stevens High School. Predicting the future, her high school yearbook reads, "She is very likely to become a stage or screen star." Her uncle George encouraged her to go to acting school. At the age of 18, she was accepted at the American Academy of

Grace Kelly's graduation portrait from the American Academy of Dramatic Arts

Dramatic Arts in New York. She moved to New York City and lived on her own. At the academy, she began to develop acting skills that she would later perfect. It wasn't easy. She learned to avoid speaking through her nose. She lost her Philadelphia accent and learned to use an "all-American" style of speech. For Grace, this school was like a dream come true. She was doing what she loved most of all.

Coming from a family of achievers, Grace was determined to succeed. She wanted to be an independent woman with a career, just like her mother. She didn't want to depend on her parents for money. To make ends meet at school, Grace did some modeling. Like her mother, she didn't pursue it seriously. Acting was what Grace wanted to do. After she graduated from drama school in 1949, acting roles started coming her way.

Worthington Miner directs Grace in her first television appearance for the "Studio One" production of *The Rockingham Tea Set.*

2

The Start of a Career

Soon after graduating, Grace landed parts in two plays at Bucks County Playhouse in Pennsylvania, in *The Heiress* and her uncle George's play *The Torch Bearers*. This acting experience put her in the public eye and led to her getting a role on Broadway in Strindberg's play *The Father*. Critics found her convincing as the daughter. The *New York Times* called her performance "charming." But the reviews found the rest of the company's performances weak, and the play closed after a short run.

It wasn't easy making a career as a stage actress. Except for *The Father* and a comedy called *To Be Continued*, Grace lost every Broadway part she auditioned for. It was disappointing. But Worthington Miner, president of the American Academy of Dramatic Arts, remembered her from her school productions. He was directing television dramas, and he asked Grace to try out for *The Rockingham Tea Set.* In January 1950, she appeared in that CBS drama series. She played a young nurse caring for a bitter, disabled woman.

When Grace entered what was then the new field of television, she became an instant success. At the time, most people relied on radios for news and entertainment. Americans were just starting to buy their first television sets around 1950. Television screens were only 12 inches across, and the picture was black and white. Most contemporary television shows are videotaped, edited, and then played on the air at a later time. Few programs are live, except news, sports events, and award shows. In the 1950s, however, all TV programs were broadcast live—the performance took place as the viewer watched. Grace felt at home on live TV; it was almost like being onstage. Television audiences could spot any mistakes even more clearly than theater audiences. Television needed actors who could handle the pressure of live theater, where everything had to be perfect. Grace Kelly was good at that.

She became a familiar face on TV. Grace had many lead roles on the weekly "Philco/Goodyear Playhouse." She played Ann Rutledge, President Lincoln's first love, and starred in *The Way of an Eagle* as Mrs. John Audubon. (John Audubon was a bird expert who identified and painted many American birds.)

Grace played the lead in *The Big Build-Up* on the "Hallmark Hall of Fame." In her role as the starlet Clare Conroy, she had a line that held true for her own life at the time: "I would rather be hungry and be an actress than anything else in the world."

Her television experience helped Grace improve her acting. From 1950 to 1951, she acted in at least 60 television programs, including "Kraft Television Theater" and "Suspense." Because Grace was determined to become a successful actress, she played a variety of parts. She even sang and danced on Ed Sullivan's television program, a popular, weekly variety show.

Grace used her experience on TV as a stepping stone to becoming a movie star. Hollywood producers noticed her television performances. Other actors such as James Dean and Paul Newman joined Grace Kelly as the first television actors to succeed in film.

Grace's first movie role was a small part in a drama called *Fourteen Hours*. Like the Broadway play *The Father*, the film was not a hit with critics. But Grace's performance in the movie made people notice her. One teenager in Oregon liked Grace's first movie so much that she formed a Grace Kelly fan club.

In the summer of 1951, Grace Kelly was thrilled when she was asked to return to the stage. This time she performed with the Elitch Gardens Stock Company, a theater company in Denver, Colorado. She learned 10 different roles to be acted in 11 weeks. She starred

In the western movie *High Noon,* Grace played opposite Gary Cooper.

in *The Detective Story, Legend of Sarah, The Man Who Came to Dinner,* and *Ring Around the Moon.* But before she could finish the season at Elitch, she was offered a starring part in a western film that is now a classic—*High Noon.*

In the film, Grace, who was just 22 years old, played opposite Gary Cooper, a legendary actor. She was his young Quaker bride, who wanted him to give up gun fighting. Cooper taught her many things she didn't know about acting. In a theater, for example, an actor must use big, sweeping movements and dramatic expressions so that the audience sitting in the back seats as well as those in the front row can understand what's happening onstage. But in the movies, a camera can come up close and record even a tiny expression. It's more like real life. Grace said that Gary Cooper taught her the difference between stage acting and film acting. She told a reporter from *Motion Picture* magazine, "On the stage you have to emote not only for the front rows, but for the balcony too, and I'm afraid I overdid it. He taught me that the camera is always in the front row, and how to take it easy."

Coming to Hollywood and movie stardom didn't faze Grace. Her life-style remained simple. She shared a one-bedroom Hollywood apartment with another actress. She even made some of her own clothes. When she wasn't working, Grace studied dance, voice, music, and art.

By 1952 Grace's career was soaring. She was chosen for the film *Mogambo*, in which she played an aristocratic English woman who goes on a safari to hunt big game with her husband. For her role, Grace needed to speak with a slight English accent. Her voice lessons were put to use and her accent was perfect.

Mogambo starred two other Hollywood legends, Ava Gardner and Clark Gable. The filming was done in Kenya, in Africa. Grace took Swahili lessons before leaving so she would be able to talk to the Africans

Grace with actor Donald Sinden in *Mogambo*

she hoped to meet. While on location, she became good friends with her costars. In the actors' tents, Grace lifted spirits by using her talent for accents and imitation to tell jokes that kept everyone laughing. Making *Mogambo* widened Grace's world. She traveled through thousands of miles of African country that had never been filmed before. She told *Time* magazine, "I wanted *Mogambo* for three things: John Ford [the director], Clark Gable, and a free trip to Africa."

This big-budget production introduced Grace's talent to moviegoers throughout the United States. She was nominated for an Academy Award as best

Grace Kelly, Hollywood star

supporting actress. In the United States, an Oscar
(the gold-plated statuette given annually by the
Academy of Motion Picture Arts and Sciences) is the
most important award for filmmaking. Although she
didn't win the Oscar, she felt honored just to be
considered for the prize. After *Mogambo* Grace could
choose which roles she wanted to play.

Cary Grant and Grace Kelly attended the premiere of *To Catch a Thief* in Philadelphia.

3

Stardom

Alfred Hitchcock, a great English director, also noticed Grace Kelly. He wanted her for a leading role in *Dial M for Murder*. She played a woman who manages to escape a murder plot. Hitchcock was very impressed by Grace's professional attitude. She always arrived on time, knew her lines, and worked long hours without complaint. Movie crews respected her for these qualities.

Hitchcock chose Grace again to star in *Rear Window*. In this suspenseful movie, she costarred with James Stewart, a leading actor. As far as Hitchcock was concerned, only Grace would do for the part of the sophisticated career woman. Because she was filming *Rear Window*, Grace had to refuse a role opposite Marlon Brando in *On the Waterfront*. Eva Marie Saint took the part and won an Oscar for best supporting actress. Despite this lost opportunity, *Rear Window* gave Grace's career a boost. The name Grace Kelly appeared as large as those of James Stewart and Alfred Hitchcock on the marquees at movie theaters. Some marquees displayed only her name.

A short time later, Grace made a movie called *The Bridges at Toko-Ri*. The film was about the Korean War, and Grace played the wife of a pilot about to go into battle. At this point in her career, Grace was in great demand by filmmakers, and the name "Grace Kelly" was becoming a household word.

By the age of 25, Grace was the most popular actress in the United States. People flocked to the movies to see her. The January 31, 1955, issue of *Time* magazine featured Grace Kelly on the cover. The article inside said, "In Hollywood, producers fight over her, directors beg for her, writers compose special scripts for her." Praising her acting, the article ended by saying that Grace Kelly "may yet become an authentic jewel in Hollywood's tinsel crown." *Life, Look, Ladies' Home Journal* and other magazines also put her picture on their covers.

As her popularity increased, Grace Kelly made the most important film of her career. In *The Country Girl*, a movie made in just six weeks, she gave her best performance as an unfulfilled, unhappy woman. Considering Grace's personal happiness, it must have been a difficult role for her to play.

Scenes from *Dial M for Murder*, above, *The Country Girl*, right, and *Rear Window*, below.

As Grace progressed in her career, her acting got better and better. Reviews of her performance in *The Country Girl* were excellent. A *New York Times* article said that Grace "will get her share of praise for the quality she put into her role." *Look* magazine said she performed with "compassion and psychological insight reaching the best traditions of dramatic skill." She received the New York Film Critics Award as well as the Oscar for best actress.

Immediately after she completed *The Country Girl*, Grace flew to Colombia, a country in South America. Her next movie, *Green Fire*, was an adventure story about emerald mining.

By the time *Green Fire* was completed, Grace was exhausted. But she could not rest. Alfred Hitchcock needed her in Europe for the filming of *To Catch a Thief*. Hitchcock was already on the set, waiting for her. Any delays in filming make a movie more expensive. The crew that works on a movie must be paid, regardless of whether the film is rolling.

Under this pressure, she flew from South America to Europe. But in the 1950s, such a flight was quite an ordeal. There were no direct flights from one part of the world to another. Airplanes were smaller, less powerful, and required frequent refueling. Grace was forced to make stopovers in five cities, including Paris. Her only rest was in the first-class berths of the planes, which had curtained beds. From Paris, Grace traveled to the Riviera in the south of France, where the movie was being shot.

Cary Grant, Grace's costar in *To Catch a Thief*, told a writer for the *Ladies' Home Journal* that he didn't even notice how tired she was. That was proof of her professionalism. He was also impressed by her talent. He compared her acting to the dancing of Fred Astaire—he made it seem easy, effortless. Grant said that, "From the actor's point of view she was so easy to work with, it was a delight. . . . From the director's point of view she knew her business. . . . She did her job well and she saved the studio money."

By this time, Grace felt very comfortable working with "Hitch." She told Hitchcock biographer Donald Spoto, "I learned a tremendous amount about motion-picture making . . . he [Hitchcock] gave me a great deal of confidence in myself." In *To Catch a Thief*, Grace played an American heiress. Hitchcock created a costume ball scene so he could show Grace wearing a shimmering gold silk gown.

Grace Kelly had a good time making *To Catch a Thief*. The Riviera is a beautiful area. Its beaches lie on the *Côte d'Azur* (the sky-blue coast), on the Mediterranean Sea. The lower Alps rise behind the coastline. Throughout the area are small museums and medieval villages. Grace enjoyed dining in wonderful restaurants with spectacular views and delicious food.

Grace received the Oscar for best actress of 1954 for her role in *The Country Girl*.

Monaco, a small country occupying only about three quarters of a square mile (1.9 square kilometers), is also located on the Riviera. Monaco is a principality, which means it is ruled by a prince. The people there speak French. While filming *To Catch a Thief*, Grace visited Monaco. She loved flowers and had heard of the country's beautiful gardens, especially those of Prince Rainier, its ruler.

Prince Rainier III lives and rules from Monaco's palace, perched on cliffs overlooking the Mediterranean. This is unusual in modern times. Most monarchs are symbols or figureheads who have no real power. Prince Rainier's family, the Grimaldis,

The palace is located in the center of Monaco's old town, pictured above.

Grace starred in *The Swan,* with Alec Guiness.

To Catch a Thief, with Cary Grant, was filmed on the Riviera near Monaco.

have reigned since 1297. In fact, part of the palace was built in the 1200s.

After 1861, Monaco developed the town of Monte Carlo into a popular gambling resort. It was a profitable decision—Monaco became one of the richest nations in the world. Grace went to the glamorous Monte Carlo Casino, but when *To Catch a Thief* was completed, she returned to the United States without having met the prince.

Soon after her return, however, the French government invited her back to the Riviera to represent the

United States at the Cannes Film Festival, where the most important French film awards are presented. Grace felt proud to have *The Country Girl* shown at the festival.

Prince Rainier, who was a big fan of Grace's, issued an invitation for her to visit the palace. Her fans so overwhelmed her in Cannes, however, that she almost canceled the palace meeting. Both she and the prince were busy with obligations, and the visit had to be rescheduled. But finally Grace arrived. Rainier showed her his garden. She also saw his small zoo, including two lions, a tiger, panthers, a bear, and a variety of monkeys. Grace told Pierre Galante, the photographer who arranged their meeting, that Prince Rainier "reached inside the cage and petted a tiger."

Grace thought the prince was "so very charming." Prince Rainier thought Grace was gentle and elegant. He told her that he planned to visit the United States soon and would like to see her there. She was very pleased.

In the summer of 1955, Grace returned to the United States to make the film *The Swan*. Most of it was shot at the Biltmore Estate in Asheville, North Carolina. Interestingly enough, Grace played a princess in the movie. At the same time, she was getting letters and phone calls from a real prince.

4

The Royal Wedding

When Prince Rainier of Monaco and Grace Kelly fell in love, the news made headlines around the world. The couple was mobbed by fans and reporters wherever they went. Every detail of their lives was examined.

A prince usually marries a woman who is descended from a royal family. Grace, however, had grandparents who were poor Irish immigrants. She was not a princess. Nor was she from Monaco, or even from France. But Prince Rainier and Grace Kelly decided to marry anyway. It was a bold decision in 1955.

During all this excitement, Grace found time to make a movie called *High Society*. The musical comedy adaptation of *The Philadelphia Story* also starred Frank Sinatra, Bing Crosby, and Louis Armstrong. Grace played a spoiled rich girl. She proved the versatility of her talent in this movie, which called for comedy and singing as well as drama. She even won a Gold Record Award for the Cole Porter song "True Love," which she sang with Bing Crosby. Eventually so many records were sold that the song went platinum. (The Recording Industry Association of America gave Gold Record awards to single records that earned $1 million and Platinum Record awards to those that earned $2 million or more.)

While Grace was filming *High Society*, she began to prepare for her wedding, which turned out to be the social event of the decade. She consulted her studio's costume designer about her wedding dress. She chose a hair stylist who would accompany her to

In *High Society*, Grace hurriedly leaves a party with Frank Sinatra.

Prince Rainier and Grace posed for a favorite photographer in 1955—prior to the official public announcement of their engagement.

Monaco for the occasion. She also studied French and the history of Monaco.

Fans, the press, and friends flooded into Monaco to see the famous movie star who was about to become a real-life princess. Grace, her family, and her bridal party traveled to Monaco on the USS *Constitution*, a large ocean liner. When they arrived in Monaco's harbor eight days later, on April 12, 1956, they were greeted by a shower of red and white carnations dropped onto the ship by plane. Red and white are the colors of Monaco's flag.

The weather was cloudy and gray, but the moment Grace stepped off the boat, a wind blew away the clouds and the sun began to shine. On the Riviera, a strong wind called the mistral blows down from the Alps. Stories have been told for centuries about the mistral.

During the wedding trip to Monaco, *top*, Grace relaxed with her parents aboard the U.S.S. *Constitution*. When the ship arrived, Prince Rainier welcomed the future princess to Monaco.

Monaco's beautiful harbor

The mistral probably caused the dramatic weather change when Grace arrived, but ever since then, a quick change from clouds to bright sun in Monaco has been called "Grace Kelly weather."

Rainier romanced his bride-to-be as only a prince can. Citizens of Monaco lined the harbor to see her arrival. Fireworks were launched. Another plane dropped thousands of small U.S. and Monégasque flags. Finally, there was a 21-gun salute. All lampposts were decorated with flags bearing the intertwined letters *R* and *G*, for Rainier and Grace. At one of the prewedding dinner parties, several entertainers performed. The final performance was by a magician who produced 12 white doves from his ears, fingertips, and shirt buttons. The chandeliers were then turned off to show fireworks outside the window. The intertwined initials *R* and *G* were created by fireworks.

In royal fashion, guests received a souvenir program for the evening. In addition to listing the entertainment, it contained a love story written for Grace and Rainier by the famous French author Jean Cocteau. After the festivities, Prince Rainier and Grace escaped to a waiting limousine to avoid the throngs of reporters and photographers.

The following night, after their guests had left a festive but small dinner party at the palace, Rainier took Grace and a few close friends to the beautiful town of Eze-Village. Perched high on a mountain, Eze boasts one of the best views of the Mediterranean. Because they returned late, Grace got little sleep before another busy day of luncheons, meetings, and ceremonies.

On Wednesday, April 18, Grace and Prince Rainier were married in a civil ceremony, the official state wedding. There Grace Kelly became a princess. But the religious ceremony was yet to come—on the following day.

The wedding brought much of the world together. Nine countries televised the wedding to more than 30 million viewers. In 1956, when television was still new, an audience that size was incredible. People from 31 nations attended the celebration. Grace's movie studio, MGM, filmed the big event, and called it *The Wedding of the Century.*

Presents arrived from people all around the world.

The royal couple celebrated with Mr. and Mrs. Kelly, Sally Parish Richardson, *far left,* and Carolyn Scott Reybold, *far right.* Notice the miniature palace at the base of the wedding cake.

Queen Elizabeth of England sent a solid gold tray. Mr. and Mrs. Cary Grant gave them an antique desk. Prince Rainier gave Grace a diamond necklace and tiara. As part of a contest, thousands of French children wrote poems to Grace.

Prince Rainier himself had designed the uniform he wore at the religious wedding ceremony. It mixed French and Italian military history, since Monaco was influenced by both. Grace Kelly wore a silk wedding dress. The Valenciennes lace on her ivory-colored gown was 125 years old. Real pearls decorated her cap and dress.

A view of the Mediterranean Sea from the town of Eze

The wedding took place in Monaco's cathedral. Besides a maid of honor, Grace had six bridesmaids, four flower girls, and two pages who carried the wedding rings on a satin pillow. After Grace and Rainier exchanged vows and rings, a mass was celebrated. A choir sang, and the Monte Carlo Philharmonic Orchestra provided the music. After the ceremony, the wedding party, led by Their Serene Highnesses the Prince and Princess of Monaco, drove through the streets of their tiny country to greet the thousands of waiting people.

Parts of the palace in Monaco were built in the 13th century. Canons stand outside its walls.

At the wedding reception, everything was spectacular, down to the last detail. The guests enjoyed an unusual six-tiered wedding cake. Each tier showed a scene, created with sugar, from Monaco's history. The huge base was decorated with three-dimensional sugar replicas of the palace. Two cherubs holding a gold crown stood on top of the cake.

For their honeymoon, Grace and Rainier sailed to Corsica, an island in the Mediterranean between southeastern France and northwestern Italy.

Princess Grace wore this 19th-century costume for the Centennial Ball in 1966.

5

A Princess

The Monégasques were so proud to have Grace as their princess that they created many stamps with her picture on them. Stamp collectors know that Monaco's beautiful stamps are like tiny prints of artwork. When a rose, carnation, and orchid were named in honor of Princess Grace, Monaco printed stamps of the flowers also. In Monte Carlo, near the center of town, an avenue was given the name Princess Grace.

As with each part she had played in films, Grace wanted to do the best job she could as a princess. She had to learn to speak French perfectly since it was her new country's language. But what does a princess really do? Grace of Monaco decided to help other people.

Her first big assignment came when Prince Rainier asked her to take over his job as leader of Monaco's

Some children visited with Princess Grace at the Garderie de Fatima, a nursery school in Monaco.

Red Cross. If there is a disaster somewhere in the world, the Red Cross helps the people affected. Grace and Rainier donated their profits from *The Wedding of the Century* to the Red Cross. To raise more money, Grace held costume balls similar to the ball scene in *To Catch a Thief*. People from all over the world, including many Hollywood friends, attended the balls. Grace also encouraged people to volunteer their time to the Red Cross. She began a junior branch for young people.

She arranged for volunteers to visit old or disabled people who couldn't leave their homes. Sometimes Princess Grace herself visited. Through the Red Cross she even founded a home for retired people, the Residence Cap-Fleuri.

Grace was struck by the fact that there were no day-care centers for the children of working mothers in Monaco. Ahead of her time, she established a day-care center through the Red Cross.

Grace became honorary president of the World Association of Friends of Children (L'Association Mondiale des Amis de L'Enfance in French, also called AMADE). She was one of its founders. Grace gave a speech in French saying, "AMADE was born . . . with no other strength than its founders' will to succeed. Its cradle is the smallest country in the world. But it means to grow from frontier to frontier, covering the earth with a network of true friends of children." AMADE helps children who are poor or sick, providing medicine and food. AMADE speaks out against problems children face—such as poverty, hunger, sickness, and neglect.

Grace couldn't reach some people who needed help because their problems weren't covered by Red Cross or AMADE services. She decided to start her own aid group—the Princess Grace Foundation. She set up stores to sell jewelry, paintings, and pottery made by Monaco's artists. She even sold her own handiwork there—such as a scarf she had designed. The stores' earnings go directly to the foundation while the artists earn money by selling their creations. The foundation uses its money to provide scholarships for young artists to attend art schools.

Princess Grace also helped a famous entertainer who lived in the region. The African-American dancer and singer Josephine Baker had won the hearts of the French people in Paris music halls. Baker was honored by the French government for her work with the Resistance during World War II. (The Resistance was an underground organization that worked against the Nazis when they occupied France.) After the war, Josephine Baker adopted 12 orphaned children from all over the world. Despite her enormous success as an entertainer, Baker went into debt. She had spent all her money on a castle she bought for her children, but she couldn't afford to maintain it. She and her family were about to become homeless when Princess Grace helped by finding a new, more affordable home for them near Monaco.

Prince Rainier and Princess Grace had three children: Princess Caroline, born on January 23, 1957; Prince Albert, born on March 14, 1958; and Princess Stephanie, born on February 1, 1965. The royal family lived in the palace or in their nearby country home, Roc Agel. Many people were surprised that the royal children were delivered by natural childbirth, with no medication. Grace insisted on it. When she also decided to breast-feed, or nurse, her children, she sent shock waves through the aristocracy and much of the United States. In the 1950s, most babies were bottle-fed because it was thought to be modern and more convenient. In Europe an aristocrat usually had a wet nurse, a woman who was hired to breast-feed babies.

Princess Grace helped singer Josephine Baker find a home for her 12 adopted children.

Grace felt so strongly about breast-feeding her children that she became an important spokesperson for the La Leche League. This group teaches new parents about the importance of nursing babies. Nursing provides better nourishment for babies and helps form a bond between mother and child.

Grace's most important job was to reign as princess of her people. Monaco is a wealthy country, but Grace still tried to improve it. She had a swimming pool built for the citizens of Monaco. The hospital of Monaco was renamed for Princess Grace when a new wing was added. She thought it needed flowers, pictures, and other decorations to cheer the patients, so she raised the necessary money and also decorated the hospital.

Grace wanted to get to know the people of Monaco. She invited families to dinner at the palace. She established a Christmas party tradition that was a big success. All the children of Monaco were invited to the palace for a party every year. Princess Grace and her royal family entertained the children in the throne room with magic, a movie, and clowns. Each child also received a present.

Sometimes Grace found it difficult to be a princess— the symbol of a country. Not only were the customs of a foreign country different, but royal customs and behavior required great formality. For example, women who were invited to the palace for lunch had to wear hats. As an American, a foreigner, Grace often felt

Prince Rainier, Princess Stephanie, Prince Albert, Princess Caroline, and Princess Grace distributed presents to the children of Monaco at the annual palace Christmas party.

President Charles de Gaulle and Madame de Gaulle visited Prince Rainier and Princess Grace at the palace in Monaco.

that she had to prove herself to her citizens, who expected her to be perfect. She did, however, change the hat rule.

When she traveled, Grace represented the principality of Monaco. The charm and poise she had developed as an actress served her well as a princess-ambassador. Because Monaco is almost surrounded by France, the two nations must cooperate. Princess Grace was a good diplomat. Even the French president, Charles de Gaulle, admired her.

Back in the United States, Grace's stature was raised to a new level. Now she was royalty. Her story was living proof of the American dream. Although she gave up her American citizenship, people often called her an American princess.

The Irish, too, were proud of her, since her father's family was from Ireland. A near riot was caused by her visit there in 1961. She eventually bought the Kelly family cottage in County Mayo, Ireland. Always seeking more information, Grace bought hundreds of books about her Irish homeland. She enjoyed exploring her roots.

When Grace became Monaco's princess, she was required to give up her career as an actress. She seriously considered taking the lead in *Marnie*, an Alfred Hitchcock film, but the citizens of Monaco disapproved. Accepting her duty to her people, Grace turned down the role and told the newspaper *Nice-Matin*, "I have been very influenced by the reaction which the announcement provoked in Monaco." Her real-life role as princess of Monaco was more important to her than acting.

But Grace remained close to her former profession through activities in Monaco. The International Television Festival, held in Monaco, was created by Princess Grace. Like the Cannes Film Festival, the International Television Festival judges TV productions from all over the world. Grace also made two American television documentaries about Monaco.

Monaco has its own television channel, which is seen in France and Italy. The station's programming shows Grace's influence. Although the principality is French-speaking, occasionally television programs—

especially American films— are broadcast in English.

Grace also encouraged the development of theater in Monaco. The Monte Carlo Theater had not been used since before World War II, and it was in poor condition. Some plays were held in the Opera House, but they were difficult to schedule between concerts. Because Grace loved acting, she wanted plays to be easily performed in her country. Grace and Rainier had a new theater built and chose the decorations. Grace understood lighting and stage materials, so she ordered the best. Prince Rainier secretly arranged to name the playhouse the Princess Grace Theater. It was founded in 1981.

Monaco is a modern cultural center that attracts entertainers from around the world. Grace's friends in the entertainment world liked to visit during Monaco's springtime festival, the Printemps des Arts de Monte Carlo. The festival begins in mid-April and lasts until the middle of May. Dance, opera, and music are performed.

Grace dreamed about but never pursued a career in ballet. While searching for a place for young Princess Caroline and Princess Stephanie to study ballet, Grace found a school in need of financial support. Its founder was Marika Besobrasova, a Russian ballet teacher. Because the Princess Grace Foundation provided financial support to the school, it took the name Académie de Danse Classique Princesse Grace.

An evening of ballet at the Academy de Danse featured Princess Caroline, at the center of the dance, and Princess Stephanie with hands crossed, to Caroline's right.

Besobrasova and Grace of Monaco helped the school's reputation grow. Together they attracted talented dancers to the school by offering scholarships from the foundation. The Monaco school ranks with those of the Royal Ballet in London and the Paris Opera Ballet. Besobrasova recalls that on one occasion, Princess Grace herself applied the children's makeup for a dress rehearsal.

Princess Grace told the story of another ballet school in *The Children of Theater Street*, a movie about the study of ballet in Russia. Grace wrote most of the script herself and also narrated the movie. *The Children of Theater Street* was nominated for an Oscar as best documentary. The Film Advisory Board gave Princess Grace the Award of Excellence for her narration.

The Twentieth Century-Fox film studio elected Grace of Monaco to a seat on its board. Business decisions made by the board included choosing what movies to produce. When she accepted the position, she was the only woman on the board. Grace became actively involved and her artistic judgment was valuable. Although she couldn't be in front of the movie camera, Grace enjoyed working behind the scenes.

In 1968 Grace started the Garden Club of Monaco. She encouraged people from different backgrounds to join the club. Anyone who loved flowers could join. The garden club presents an annual May flower show at which men and women compete in flower-arranging contests. Even Prince Rainier entered — and won. He used a pseudonym, or fictitious name, so that judges wouldn't know who he was and favor his arrangement. Because of Grace and her club, Monaco became an international center for flower arranging. She also co-wrote *My Book of Flowers*, which contains photos of the pressed-flower collages she made.

Grace was very busy in her role as a princess. She rose at 7:00 A.M. and usually made breakfast for her family, and then worked throughout the day. Fundraising often involved evening parties, so her work sometimes lasted late into the night. She had very little free time. But in Scotland, a famous American was needed to read poetry, so she accepted the request.

In 1976 the Edinburgh Arts Festival organized a bicentennial salute to the United States, which was celebrating its 200th birthday as a nation. Princess

Princess Grace enjoyed working on pressed-flower collages.

Grace agreed to read some poetry at the festival. "Wild Peaches" by American poet Elinor Wylie required a Southern accent, and Grace enjoyed the challenge. Judith Balaban Quine, Grace's close friend and a bridesmaid at her wedding, wrote that through the poetry readings, Grace "was in fact acting again." It became one of her artistic outlets.

She also read some of Shakespeare's sonnets and selections from *Twelfth Night* in Stratford-upon-Avon, Shakespeare's birthplace. That performance, too, was a success and a testimony to her talent.

Grace then toured the United States in 1978 with a whole new program. She combined poetry and prose in a program called "Birds, Beasts, and Flowers." The World Wildlife Fund received the money she earned on tour. While benefiting wildlife, she also encouraged people to read poetry.

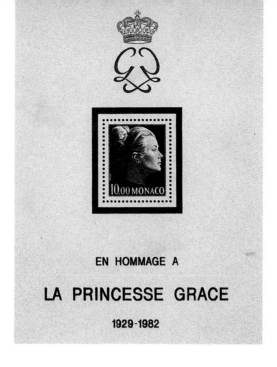

EN HOMMAGE A

LA PRINCESSE GRACE

1929-1982

◩ ◩ ◩

Driving in some parts of the Riviera can be dangerous. Many roads are narrow with single lanes. Traffic going in the opposite direction on a mountain is only divided by a painted line. A high corniche—the road along the face of a cliff—provides beautiful views, but in a car, a peek out the window can be frightening. Many spots have steep drops—sometimes without a guard rail. On the morning of September 13, 1982, with Princess Stephanie in the car beside her, Princess Grace accidentally drove off one of these steep roads. Grace apparently suffered a stroke and then lost control of the wheel. Princess Stephanie suffered a fractured vertebra. Princess Grace died the following night.

Princess Caroline, Prince Rainier, Princess Grace, Prince Albert, and Princess Stephanie in a family portrait in 1974

6

Her Work Continues

Grace, through her work, affected many lives. Now her children carry on her job of helping people. Princess Caroline came up with the idea of a telephone hot line for Monaco's teenagers with problems. When she has time, Caroline answers the telephone herself. She also leads the Princess Grace Foundation.

Prince Albert is training to rule Monaco. Like his grandfather, he is athletic and participates in the Olympics. He is also the youngest member of the International Olympics Committee, which organizes the event.

Much like her mother, Princess Stephanie has modeled and designed clothing. She has also performed as a singer in Europe. Her first American release contains a song, "Words Upon the Wind," that is dedicated to Princess Grace. One line of the song says of Grace, "You're a part of me."

Prince Albert was the captain of Monaco's bobsled team and a member of the International Olympic Committee in 1992.

Princess Stephanie hosted the Princess Grace Foundation-USA Junior Endowment Benefit in New York in 1991.

Princess Grace had dreamed of recreating Monte Carlo's ballet company. Early in the 20th century, the ballet company had flourished. From 1911 until his death in 1929, Sergei Diaghilev, one of the most famous names in ballet, choreographed and performed his new ballets in Monte Carlo. In 1922 Monte Carlo became the permanent base for Diaghilev's Ballet Russe. But the ballet company never regained its splendor after Diaghilev's death.

Princess Caroline joined Monaco's Youth March in October 1978.

Grace wanted to revive the ballet, but she didn't live to see another dance company based in Monte Carlo. Because of her earlier efforts, however, and with the help of Princess Caroline, Monaco finally got its own company in 1984. The Ballet de Monte Carlo and the Académie de Danse Classique Princesse Grace attract ballet students from around the world.

Grace Kelly's life has been called a fairy tale. But it was through hard work that she achieved goals for

At a poetry reading in 1978, Princess Grace shared the stage with Richard Pasco of the Royal Shakespeare Company.

herself and her causes. She symbolized motherhood by her loving attention to her family and the children of the world. Not content to rest among her riches, Grace chose to enrich the lives of others. Monaco and the world remember her with love. Through her work, Princess Grace spread happiness ever after.

ACKNOWLEDGMENTS

The following photographs are reproduced through the courtesy of the Princess Grace Foundation-USA: p. 2 (F. Picedi); p. 8 (Jean-Marie Mole); p. 13; p. 20; p. 32, (Paramount Pictures Corporation); pp. 34 and 37 (Howell Conant); p. 41; pp. 44, 46, 50, 51 (G. Lukomski); p. 49 (Hoe); p. 54 (René Briano); p. 56; pp. 58, 64, and front cover (Gianni Bozzacchi); p. 60 (Gaetan Luci); p. 62 (Juroll); p. 63.

Additional photographs are reproduced through the courtesy of: the Academy of Motion Picture Arts and Sciences, p. 23; American Academy of Dramatic Arts, pp. 15, 16 (Irving Haberman); p. 61 © 1991 (Adam Scull) Globe Photos, Inc.; Hollywood Book and Poster, p. 27 (all); James L. McGuire. p. 57; Monaco Government Tourist and Convention Bureau, pp. 31 (bottom), 43; Movie Star News, p. 30; Karen Sirvaitis, p. 39; Elizabeth Surcouf, p. 42; Urban Archives, Temple University, Philadelphia, PA, pp. 11, 14, 24; p. 22 © 1953, p. 31 (top) © 1956, p. 36 © 1956, Turner Entertainment Co. All rights reserved; the Bettmann Archive, pp. 12, 38 (both). Back flap photo by Joan DeBellis.